COOL WRITTEN RECORDS

The Proof Is in the Paper

Esther Beck

ABDO
Publishing Company

Visit us at www.abdopublishing.com

Published by ABDO Publishing Company, 8000 West 78th Street, Edina, Minnesota 55439.

Printed in the United States.
Design and Production: Mighty Media, Inc.
Art Direction: Kelly Doudna
Photo Credits: Kelly Doudna, Ablestock, iStockPhoto (Christine Balderas, Susan Daniels, Pawel Kaminski, Stefan Klein), ShutterStock
Series Editor: Pam Price

Library of Congress Cataloging-in-Publication Data

Beck, Esther.
Cool written records : the proof is in the paper / Esther Beck.
p. cm. -- (Cool CSI)
Includes index.
ISBN 978-1-60453-488-7
1. Legal documents--Identification--Juvenile literature. 2. Writing--Identification--Juvenile literature. 3. Forensic science--Juvenile literature. I. Title.

HV8074.B43 2009
363.25'65--dc22

2008023820

To Adult Helpers

You're invited to assist up-and-coming forensic investigators! And it will pay off in many ways. Your children can develop new skills, gain confidence, and do some interesting projects while learning about science. What's more, it's going to be a lot of fun!

These projects are designed to let children work independently as much as possible. Let them do whatever they are able to do on their own. Also encourage them to keep a CSI journal. Soon, they will be thinking like real investigators.

So get out your magnifying glass and stand by. Let your young investigators take the lead. Watch and learn. Praise their efforts. Enjoy the scientific adventure!

CONTENTS

FUN WITH FORENSICS

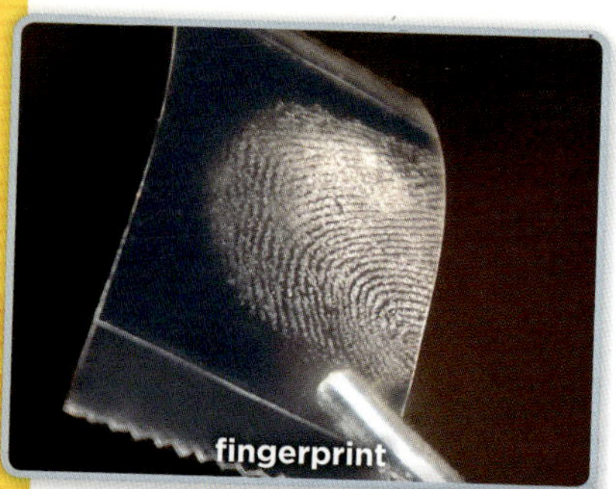
fingerprint

shoe print

fibers

So you want to know more about crime scene investigation, or CSI. Perhaps you saw a crime solvers show on television and liked it. Or maybe you read about an ace investigator in a favorite **whodunit** book. Now you're curious, how do the investigators solve crimes?

The answer is *forensic science*. This term means science as it relates to the law. The many areas of forensic science can help link people to crimes, even if there are no eyewitnesses. Forensic scientists look at the evidence left at a crime scene and try to figure out what happened there.

tool marks

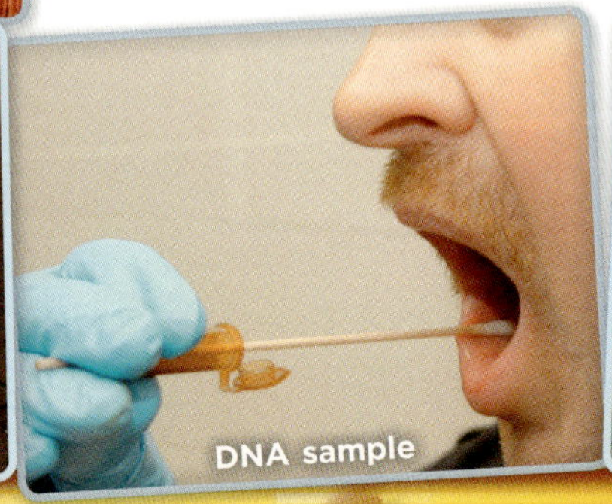
DNA sample

chemical residue

Evidence can include fingerprints, shoe prints, and fibers. It can include DNA samples from blood and saliva, tool marks, and chemical residue. Often this evidence can be quite small. In the CSI business, this is known as trace evidence. But even the smallest evidence can place a suspect at a crime scene.

Crime scene investigators **analyze** the evidence. Then they try to answer these questions about a crime.

1. What happened?
2. Where and when did it occur?
3. Who are the suspects, and why did they do it?
4. How was the crime done?

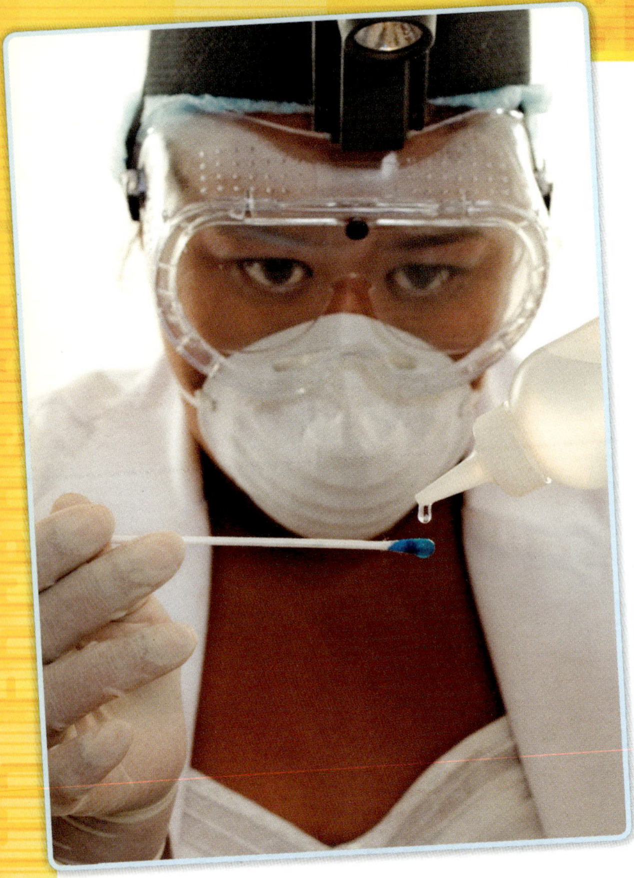

Different kinds of evidence require different kinds of scientists to find the answers to these questions. Forensic scientists specialize in fields such as chemistry, biology, physics, engineering, psychology, and even **entomology** and **botany**.

All these scientists use common sense and old-fashioned observation. They also rely on high-tech equipment and the latest scientific discoveries. Most important, forensic scientists use the scientific method.

Investigators begin by observing the crime scene. They then predict what happened and, if possible, who committed the crime based on the evidence.

Next they test the evidence. Their test results may support their predictions. Or, the results may tell them that their predictions were not correct.

Finally, they draw a conclusion about what happened. They may decide that further testing is required.

In this book series, you'll have a chance to test your own crime-solving talent. You'll do some challenging hands-on forensics activities. Each book in the series covers a specific area of CSI. In addition to this book, *Cool Written Records: The Proof Is in the Paper*, be sure to check out:

- *Cool Biological Clues: What Hair, Bones, and Bugs Tell Us*
- *Cool Crime Scene Basics: Securing the Scene*
- *Cool Eyewitness Encounters: How's Your Memory?*
- *Cool Forensic Tools: Technology at Work*
- *Cool Physical Evidence: What's Left Behind*

Altogether, these books show how crime scene investigators use science to **analyze** evidence and solve crimes.

Whoduzit in Whodunits: Forensic Psychologists

Psychologists study minds and behavior. Forensic psychologists study the minds and behavior of crime suspects. They try to determine motive, or why a person may have committed a crime. They may try to determine whether a person was sane when he or she committed a crime.

The Scientific Method

Forensic scientists aren't the only ones who use the scientific method. All scientists do.

The scientific method is a series of steps that scientists follow when trying to answer a question about how the world works. Here are the basic steps of the scientific method.

1. Observe. Pay attention to how something works.
2. Predict. Make a simple statement that explains what you observed.
3. Test. Design an experiment that tests your prediction. You need a good idea of what data to gather during the test. A good test has more than one trial and has controlled variables.
4. Conclude. Compare the data and make a conclusion. This conclusion should relate to your prediction. It will either support the prediction or tell you that your prediction was incorrect.

COOL CSI JOURNAL

Taking notes is important when you collect evidence as a crime scene investigator. Writing down facts helps crime scene investigators remember all the details of a crime scene later, when a crime is tried in court.

At the beginning of each activity in this book, there is a section called "Take Note!" It contains suggestions about what to record in your CSI journal. You can predict what you think will happen when you test evidence. And you can write down what did happen. Then you can draw a conclusion.

As you do experiments, record things in your journal. You will be working just like a real forensic scientist.

TAKE NOTE!

Get out your CSI journal when you *see* this box. "Take Note!" may have questions for you to answer about the project. There may be a suggestion about how to look at the project in a different way. There may even be ideas about how to organize the evidence you find. Your CSI journal is the place to keep track of everything!

SAFE SCIENCE

Good scientists practice safe science. Here are some important things to remember.

- Check with an adult before you begin any project. Sometimes you'll need an adult to buy materials or help you handle them for a while. For some projects, an adult will need to help you the whole time. The instructions will say when an adult should assist you.
- Ask for help if you're unsure about how to do something.
- If something goes wrong, tell an adult immediately.
- Read the list of things you'll need. Gather everything before you begin working on a project.
- Don't taste, eat, or drink any of the materials or the results unless the directions say that you can.
- Use protective gear. Scientists wear safety goggles to protect their eyes. They wear gloves to protect their hands from chemicals and possible burns. They wear aprons or lab coats to protect their clothing.
- Clean up when you are finished. That includes putting away materials and washing containers, work surfaces, and your hands.

COOL WRITTEN RECORDS: THE PROOF IS IN THE PAPER

Following a paper trail might not sound like exciting CSI work. But documents can be key evidence in solving crimes. Criminals sometimes write **ransom** notes or forge **signatures** on important business papers. Forensic document examiners review this kind of evidence,

known in the CSI biz as questioned documents. They use observation, scientific processes, and **technology** to answer important questions such as these.

1. Who wrote the document?
2. Was the document actually created when it was supposed to have been created?
3. Has the document been altered?
4. Does the handwriting match an exemplar, or sample?

Of course, every **case** is different. And how these questions are answered is what makes the work fascinating. The first step is often **analyzing** what's on a document. When examiners study handwriting, they sometimes match unknown handwriting to a known sample. And they sometimes compare two unknown samples. Either way, the work can be as straightforward as, well, cursive writing!

That's because every person has **unique** handwriting. Plus, criminals often try to disguise their writing. They might write with their opposite hands, for example. Another trick is for male criminals to "feminize" their handwriting. That is, they try to make it look prettier than usual to confuse investigators.

Questioned-document examiners also **analyze** the paper itself. They can identify different kinds and brands of papers. Sometimes they even track the paper back to the store it came from!

They are experts at analyzing inks as well. **Chromatography** is the name of the game when it comes to ink. Investigators use this scientific process to match ink samples. A match can tell them if a specific pen was used to write a note.

In some **cases**, questioned-document examiners even evaluate documents that have been destroyed. If criminals are afraid of getting caught, they might burn the evidence. If the paper is not completely ruined, an ace document examiner can still get information from it.

As you can see, there are many ways to work with written records. The activities in this book will introduce you to the science behind forensic document examination. What you learn will help you think like a real questioned-document examiner!

Whoduzit in Whodunits: Questioned-Document Examiner

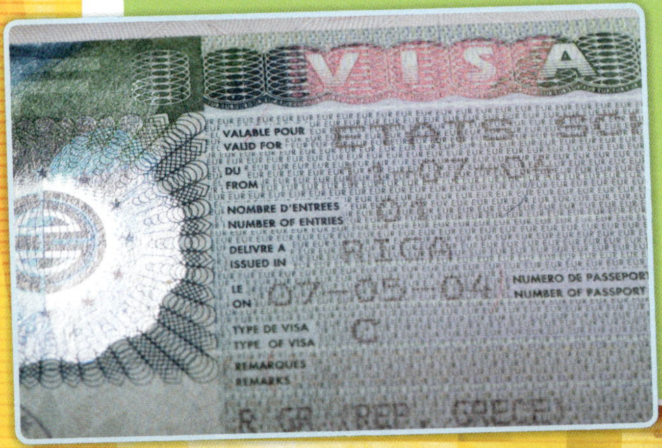

This crime scene specialist analyzes the paper trails left by criminals. A questioned-document examiner tries to determine whether a document is real. He or she looks at handwriting and **signatures**, printing, paper, and ink. Document examiners do their work in labs, far from crime scenes. That's because their work is seldom needed right away, except for documents such as **ransom** notes and bank robbery notes.

HANDWRITING 101

THE CRIME SCENE: Your best friend receives a note from a secret admirer! Of course you both want to know who it is. So you bring the note home from school. There you examine it up close, using a magnifying glass. You compare the note to stories handwritten by your classmates. These stories are your samples, or exemplars. So what does your **sleuthing** tell you?

Handwriting **analysis** is a basic skill for document examiners. In this activity, you'll try your hand at it, pardon the pun! Can you pick a handwriting match?

MATERIALS

- paper
- pens
- friends or family to create writing samples
- magnifying glass

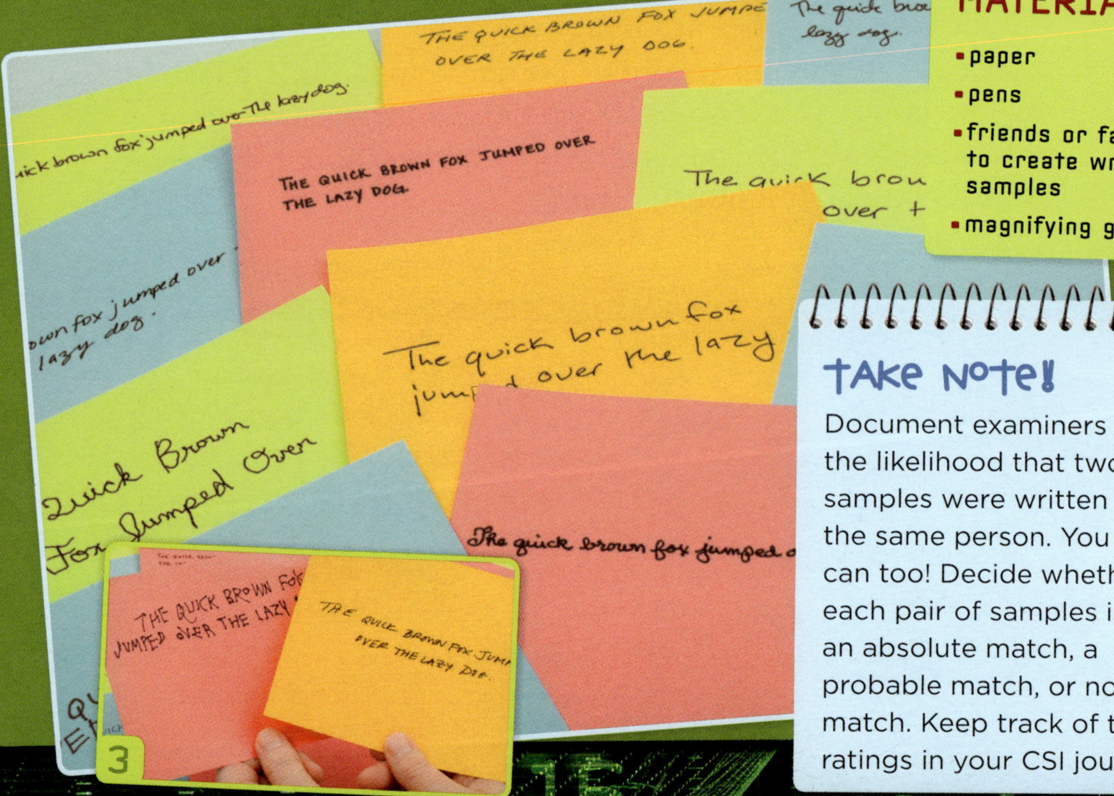

TAKE NOTE!

Document examiners rate the likelihood that two samples were written by the same person. You can too! Decide whether each pair of samples is an absolute match, a probable match, or not a match. Keep track of these ratings in your CSI journal.

1. Collect handwriting samples from family and friends. Have each person contribute two samples. They can write the same way in each sample or try to disguise their handwriting in the second sample.

2. Mix up the samples so it is not clear which samples came from which person.

3. Try matching the two samples from each writer. Use the points outlined in "Think CSI" as a guide.

4. Check your work. Have your writers verify your results.

Think CSI

Here are some of the things that document examiners consider when **analyzing** handwriting. Use these points to compare the samples in this activity.

Size and shape. Are the letters large or small? Are the letters in or out of proportion?

Slant. Do the letters slant to the left or to the right? Or, are they straight?

Spacing. Are the letters crowded together, placed widely apart, or spaced normally? How are the words spaced?

Finishing touches. Did the writer cross the t's and dot the i's?

Content. Did the writer make any grammar, punctuation, or spelling errors? Are there unique word choices?

CSI Tip

Not all evidence is handwritten. Document examiners may also be asked to analyze notes written on a typewriter or a computer. Investigators can sometimes track a sample back to a specific machine.

INVESTIGATING IMPRINTS

MATERIALS

- notebook
- pens and pencils
- friend or family member
- flashlight
- paper clips

THE CRIME SCENE: Your older brother is in trouble! He forged a note from your mom to excuse himself from gym class. But the school never even called about his note. So how does your clever mom know about it?

In this activity, you'll learn a top trade secret of CSI document examiners. See how paper indents can give away a criminal's game!

TAKE NOTE!

Write the text you decipher in your CSI notebook. Clip the original note and the indented blank page to this page. Repeat the activity using different notebooks and different pens or pencils. Have the note writer use different amounts of pressure with each sample. Can you always read the indents?

1. Have a friend or a family member write a note in the notebook. Make sure your helper uses the top piece of paper.

2. Have your helper remove the note from the notebook without showing it to you.

3. Examine the next notebook page, which should be blank. Look for indents that were made during the note writing. Can you tell what was written there? Shine a flashlight sideways across the page. Does the light help you see the indents? Another option is to lightly rub the side of a pencil tip over the indented page.

4. Write down anything you can **decipher** from the page. Compare your text with the original note. How did you do?

Think CSI

Crime scene investigators know that criminals may write and rewrite **ransom** notes. They may be trying to disguise their handwriting or deciding exactly what to say. Impressions from these attempts or from the actual note can be used as evidence. How well the impressions can be read depends on a number of factors. The thickness of the paper and how hard the writer presses are two such factors.

INK THINK

THE CRIME SCENE: Your after-school science club has a yearly science fair. Your team's project is almost finished. Then one day you find a **ransom** note in its place. Another team has played a trick on you! Fortunately, your team knows just what to do. You collect pens from each team and figure out **whodunit**.

Chromatography is a scientific process used to separate complex chemicals. In this activity, you'll use chromatography to match inks.

MATERIALS

- tape
- 3 water-soluble ink pens made by different companies but with the same color of ink
- coffee filters
- scissors
- friend or family member
- drinking glass
- water
- pencils
- piece of paper
- magnifying glass

1. Place a piece of tape on each of the pens. Number the pens 1, 2, and 3.

2. Cut the coffee filters into strips one inch (2.5 cm) wide.

3. Have your helper choose one of the pens. No peeking!

4. Don't watch as the person places a small dot of ink one inch (2.5 cm) from the bottom of a strip. Then, have him or her write *note* at the top of this strip so you can keep track of it. This strip represents the ink on the ransom note and should be set aside.

5. Continue not peeking as your helper returns the pen to the others.

6. Make dots on three more strips, using ink from a different pen on each strip. Write the number of the pen used at the top of each strip.

7. Place about ½ inch (1.3 cm) of water in a glass.

8. Start with the note ink sample. Tape the top of the strip to the middle of a pencil. Place the pencil across the top of the glass, hanging the strip in the water. The bottom of the filter strip should touch the water, but the dot should not. Leave the strip in the water for about 5 minutes. The water will seep up the strip.

9. Remove the strip from the water. Place it on the paper to dry. The pattern you see on the strip is a **chromatogram**.

8

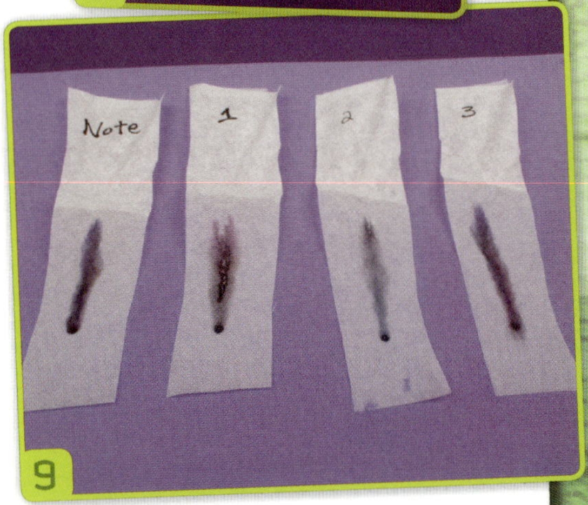

9

TAKE NOTE!

Tape the dried chromatograms in your CSI journal, along with notes such as the brand and make of each pen. Use different pens to create more chromatograms and expand your collection. How do different colors of inks appear in the chromatograms? Do inks of the same color create similar patterns? Do different brands of pens create different patterns? Do pens of the same brand create similar patterns?

11

10. Working with one strip at a time, repeat steps 8 and 9 with the remaining three strips.

11. Compare the chromatograms. Can you determine which pen was used for the **ransom** note sample?

EVEN MORE TO EXPLORE

A solvent is a liquid that can dissolve other substances. The water you used to dissolve ink is a solvent. Repeat this activity with other solvents, such as isopropyl alcohol, vinegar, or ammonia. How do your results compare?

THINK CSI

Forensic scientists are not the only ones who use **chromatography**. The process is used in many fields. Here's how it works. The chemicals in a mixture such as ink react differently to the solvent. Some will move up the filter with the water. Others will stay put.

Companies use different formulas to make their inks. So, the chromatograms for the inks vary. These differences are what make it possible to compare the chemicals. Good thinking!

PAPER CHASE

THE CRIME SCENE: Your uncle buys a box of old correspondence at an antique store. In it he finds a letter he thinks might be valuable. But is the letter really old? Fiber **analysis** can help determine the age and source of paper.

Compare paper up close using a magnifying glass or a microscope. You might be surprised by what you discover!

MATERIALS

- a variety of paper samples, including fine stationery, school notebook paper, and newspaper
- black construction paper
- magnifying glass
- scissors
- small glasses
- water
- tweezers
- slides and plastic slips
- microscope

MAGNIFIED VIEW

1. Rip a small piece from each paper sample and place it on black construction paper.

2. View each sample using the magnifying glass.

3. Describe each sample and draw a sketch of its fibers in your CSI journal.

Think CSI

Paper is made of fiber from wood and plants such as cotton, linen, and rice. Man-made fibers are sometimes included to give paper special properties. Expert document examiners use chemical tests to compare paper sources. This work is done in a forensic lab, away from the crime scene.

Take Note!

Use a table like this one to organize your notes.

	Color/description	Appearance under magnifying glass	Appearance under microscope
Stationery			
Notebook paper			
Newsprint			

MICROSCOPE VIEW

1. Cut a small square of each paper sample.

2. Place each square in its own glass of water. Soak the samples overnight.

3. Using the tweezers, remove each sample from the water and place it on a slide.

4. View the paper samples under the microscope.

5. Describe each sample and draw a sketch of its fibers in your CSI journal.

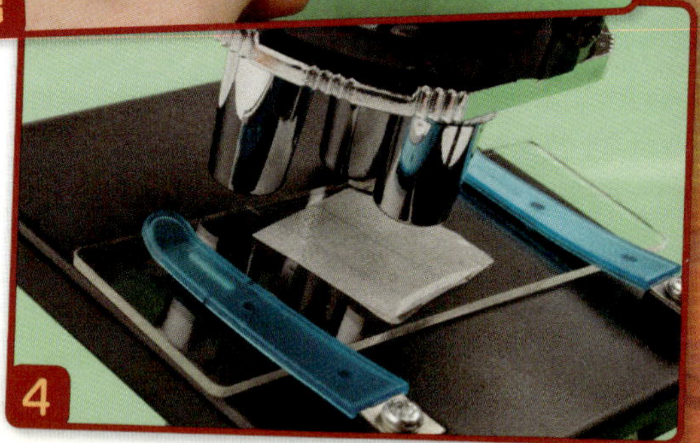

EVEN MORE TO EXPLORE

A watermark is a design that a manufacturer places on its paper. You can **see** a watermark when you hold the paper up to light. Watermarks can help examiners tell whether a document is real. For example, was this paper even available when the document was supposedly created?

Watermarks can even help determine where a certain paper was purchased. Look around your house for paper money, stationery, and other paper products that contain watermarks.

FORGERY, JUST FOR FUN!

THE CRIME SCENE: Your annoying cousins like to play pranks. They alter your school ID just for fun. They tape a picture of a monkey over your photo. Then they replace the text with silliness.

Name:
Funky Monkey

Homeroom:
ooh-ooh

Bus route:
Banana Bus

You don't notice their work. But your teacher sees your ID hanging from your backpack. He says, "Now that's some monkey business." How embarrassing!

Changing IDs and other legal papers is a crime. But practicing forgery can help a questioned-document examiner know what to look for. In this activity, you'll create member IDs for fake clubs. Then you'll trade IDs and try to copy each other's designs. Can others tell the difference between the original and the forgery?

MATERIALS

- craft supplies, including paper, glue, tape, scissors, pens
- small photos of people's heads clipped from a magazine
- friends
- computer (optional)

1. Use the craft supplies to design and create fun club IDs. Make sure to include a name, address, and photo on each ID.

2. Now exchange IDs and try copying each other's documents.

3. Review each other's work. How did you do?

TAKE NOTE!

Have you heard the saying "The more, the merrier"? Recruit friends to turn this activity into a fun game. Assign a couple of people to be questioned-document examiners. Ask the rest of the group to create IDs. Then have everyone in this group choose three IDs to copy.

The document examiners evaluate each forgery, comparing it with the sample. In their CSI journals, the examiners rate the forgeries as match or no match. The person who creates the most matches wins!

CSI Tip

One of the best ways to catch a fake or a forgery is experience. Busy document examiners develop a so-called sixth sense about when something isn't quite right. They follow up with tests to confirm their instincts.

Think CSI

IDs and other legal papers are not the only things that criminals forge. Photos, maps, books, stamps, art, and money are all targets for criminals. Document examiners call in special experts to help **analyze** rare objects. Sometimes they use powerful tools such as microscopes, X-rays, and special lights.

EVEN MORE TO EXPLORE

Take a look at a real ID, such as a driver's license or a passport. What design elements do you see that would make it difficult to copy these legal papers? Why do you think authorities add these elements to the IDs?

CONCLUSION

As you've seen, questioned-document examiners use many skills. Now that you know them, you can solve mysteries large and small. And you can continue to learn! Pay attention to how documents are used in mystery stories and crime shows on television. Track news stories in your local community. Many crimes involve illegal use of documents.

The written record offers opportunities for a creative crime solver. A keen eye, scientific know-how, and an open mind are all that are required. Then a document examiner like you can solve even the toughest **cases**. And to think it all starts with everyday paper!

GLOSSARY

analysis – the identification or study of the parts of a whole.

analyze – to study the parts of something to discover how it works or what it means.

botany – the study of plants.

case – a situation requiring investigation and consideration by police. Also, the set of arguments made by a lawyer in a court of law.

chromatogram – the pattern produced on paper or another absorbent material during chromatography.

chromatography – a process in which a chemical mixture is separated into the separate parts it is made of.

decipher – to make out the meaning of something even if it is faint or not easily recognized.

entomology – the study of bugs.

ransom – money demanded for the release of someone or something held captive.

signature – a person's name written in his or her own handwriting.

sleuth – to act like a detective and search for information.

technology – scientific knowledge used for practical purposes, especially in industry.

unique – being the only one of its kind.

whodunit – a slang word meaning detective story or mystery story.

WEB SITES

To learn more about the science of forensics, visit ABDO Publishing Company on the World Wide Web at www.abdopublishing.com. Web sites about CSI and forensics are featured on our Book Links page. These links are routinely monitored and updated to provide the most current information available.

INDEX